P9-CAO-843

A Beginning-to-Read Book

At the Pond

by Mary Lindeen

NORWOOD HOUSE PRESS

DEAR CAREGIVER, The *Beginning to Read—Read and Discover* books provide emergent readers the opportunity to explore the world through nonfiction while building early reading skills. The text integrates both common sight words and content vocabulary. These key words are featured on lists provided at the back of the book to help your child expand his or her sight word recognition, which helps build reading fluency. The content words expand vocabulary and support comprehension.

Nonfiction text is any text that is factual. The Common Core State Standards call for an increase in the amount of informational text reading among students. The Standards aim to promote college and career readiness among students. Preparation for college and career endeavors requires proficiency in reading complex informational texts in a variety of content areas. You can help your child build a foundation by introducing nonfiction early. To further support the CCSS, you will find Reading Reinforcement activities at the back of the book that are aligned to these Standards.

Above all, the most important part of the reading experience is to have fun and enjoy it!

Sincerely,

Shannon Cannon

Shannon Cannon, Ph.D.
Literacy Consultant

Norwood House Press • P.O. Box 316598 • Chicago, Illinois 60631
For more information about Norwood House Press please visit our website at
www.norwoodhousepress.com or call 866-565-2900.
© 2016 Norwood House Press. Beginning-to-Read™ is a trademark of Norwood House Press.
All rights reserved. No part of this book may be reproduced or utilized in any form or by any
means without written permission from the publisher.

Editor: Judy Kentor Schmauss
Designer: Lindaanne Donohoe

Photo Credits:

Shutterstock, cover, 1, 3, 4-5, 10-11, 12, 13, 20-21, 23, 24-25, 26-27; Dreamstime, 18-19
(©Morena696), 22 (Amberleaf); Phil Martin, 6-7, 8-9, 14-15, 16-17, 28-29

Library of Congress Cataloging-in-Publication Data
    Lindeen, Mary, author.
    At the pond / by Mary Lindeen.
        pages cm. – (A beginning to read book)
    Summary: "Take a trip to a pond. See fish, cattails, dragonflies, turtles, and other interesting plants
and animals that live there. Take a ride in the water on a canoe. You never know what you'll find
at a pond! This title includes reading activities and a word list"– Provided by publisher.
    Audience: K to grade 3
    ISBN 978-1-59953-695-8 (library edition : alk. paper)
    ISBN 978-1-60357-780-9 (ebook)
    1. Ponds–Juvenile literature. 2. Pond ecology–Juvenile literature. I. Title.
    QH541.5.P63L56 2015
    577.63'6–dc23
                                  2014047630

Manufactured in the United States of America in Stevens Point, Wisconsin. 275N–062015

Have you ever been to a pond?
It is home to many living things.

Go out on the dock.

Look down into the water.

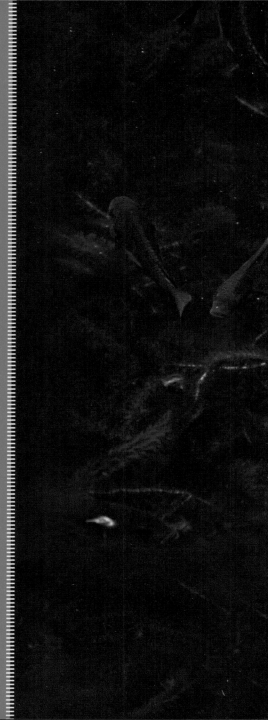

Do you see fish?

Fish live in a pond.

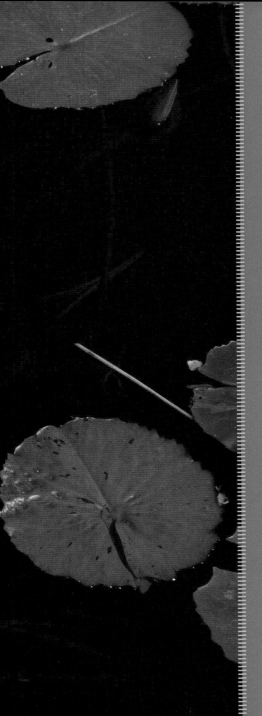

Plants live in
a pond, too.

These plants are
water lilies.

They float on the
water.

Cattails grow at the edge of a pond.

Do you think they look like a cat's tail?

Dragonflies live at a pond.

They fly over the water.

An old log is in this pond.

How many turtles do you see?

They like to sit in the sun.

Ducks are at this pond.

They swim in the water.

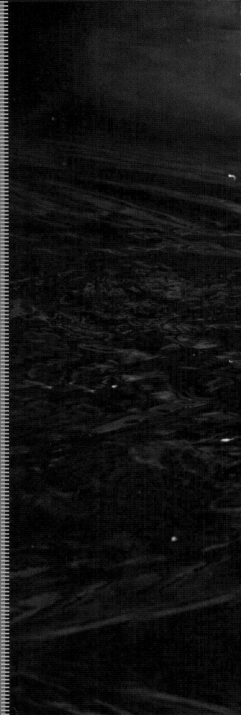

This duck has a nest by the pond.

What is in the nest?

These little eggs are frog eggs.

One day they will open.

Tadpoles will come out.

The little tadpoles
will live in the pond.

One day they will be frogs.

Frogs live in a pond.

This one is swimming.

You can get in the water, too.

Use a boat like this one.

You never know
what you will find
at a pond!

•• Reading Reinforcement ••

CRAFT AND STRUCTURE

To check your child's understanding of this book, recreate the following diagram on a sheet of paper. Read the book with your child, then help him or her fill in the diagram using what they learned. Work together to complete the diagram by writing words or ideas about a pond in the empty circles:

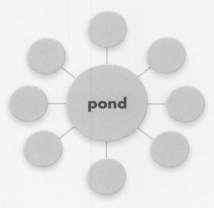

pond

VOCABULARY: Learning Content Words

Content words are words that are specific to a particular topic. All of the content words for this book can be found on page 32. Use some or all of these content words to complete one or more of the following activities:

- Help your child make word cards: On each card, have him or her write a content word, draw a picture to illustrate the word, and write a sentence using the word.

- Ask your child questions that include one or more of the content words. Each question should begin with one of these words: *who, what, when, where, why,* or *how.*

- Have your child choose a content word and draw a picture to illustrate its meaning.

- Help your child find pairs of content words that have something in common, either in meaning, structure, or both.

- Say a content word and have your child act out its meaning.

FOUNDATIONAL SKILLS: Consonant digraphs

Consonant digraphs are two consonants that together make a single sound (for example, ph in phone). Have your child identify the consonant digraphs in the list below. Then help your child find the words with consonant digraphs in this book.

cattails	sit	think	plants	what
fish	dock	eggs	ducks	they

CLOSE READING OF INFORMATIONAL TEXT

Close reading helps children comprehend text. It includes reading a text, discussing it with others, and answering questions about it. Use these questions to discuss this book with your child:

- What are two animals that live in or near a pond?
- How are turtles and ducks alike? Different?
- What would you do with a boat if you had one?
- Why do you think a cattail got its name?
- How would you combine two pond animals to make a different animal?
- Would you rather go to a swimming pool or a pond? Why?

FLUENCY

Fluency is the ability to read accurately with speed and expression. Help your child practice fluency by using one or more of the following activities:

- Reread this book to your child at least two times while he or she uses a finger to track each word as you read it.
- Read the first sentence aloud. Then have your child reread the sentence with you. Continue until you have finished this book.
- Ask your child to read aloud the words they know on each page of this book. (Your child will learn additional words with subsequent readings.)
- Have your child practice reading this book several times to improve accuracy, rate, and expression.

••• Word List •••

At the Pond uses the 76 words listed below. *High-frequency* words are those words that are used most often in the English language. They are sometimes referred to as sight words because children need to learn to recognize them automatically when they read. *Content words* are any words specific to a particular topic. Regular practice reading these words will enhance your child's ability to read with greater fluency and comprehension.

High-Frequency Words

a	do	into	old	things
an	down	is	on	think
are	find	it	one	this
at	get	know	open	to
be	go	like	out	too
been	has	little	over	use
by	have	look	see	water
can	home	many	the	what
come	how	never	these	will
day	in	of	they	you

Content Words

boat	edge	frog(s)	plants	tail
cat's	eggs	grow	pond	turtles
cattails	ever	lilies	sit	
dock	fish	live(ing)	sun	
dragonflies	float	log	swim(ing)	
duck(s)	fly	nest	tadpoles	

••• About the Author

Mary Lindeen is a writer, editor, parent, and former elementary school teacher. She has written more than 100 books for children and edited many more. She specializes in early literacy instruction and books for young readers, especially nonfiction.

••• About the Advisor

Dr. Shannon Cannon is a teacher educator in the School of Education at UC Davis, where she also earned her Ph.D. in Language, Literacy, and Culture. She serves on the clinical faculty, supervising pre-service teachers and teaching elementary methods courses in reading, effective teaching, and teacher action research.